M000015014

# Along Your Desert Journey

Robert M. Hamma

**Paulist Press**
New York/Mahwah, N.J.

The Scripture quotations herein are from the *New Revised Standard Version* Bible. Copyright © 1993 and 1989 by the Division of Christian Education of the National Council of the Churches of Christ in the U. S. A. Used by permission. All rights reserved.

Cover/book design and interior illustrations by Nicholas T. Markell.

Copyright © 1996 by Robert M. Hamma

All rights reserved. No part of this book may be reproduced or transmitted in any form or by any means, electronic or mechanical, including photocopying, recording or by any information storage and retrieval system without permission in writing from the Publisher.

Library of Congress Cataloging-in-Publication Data

Hamma, Robert M.
    Along your desert journey / Robert M. Hamma.
       p.   cm. — (IlluminationBook)
    Includes bibliographical references.
    ISBN 0-8091-3681-3 (alk. paper)
    1. Christian life—Catholic authors.  2. Wilderness (Theology)
3. Deserts—Religious aspects—Christianity.  I. Title.  II. Series:
IlluminationBooks.
BX2350.2.H29  1996
248.4—dc20                          96-26391
                                         CIP

Published by Paulist Press
997 Macarthur Boulevard
Mahwah, New Jersey 07430

Printed and bound in the
United States of America

# Contents

# IlluminationBooks
# A Foreword

*I*lluminationBooks bring to light wonderful ideas, helpful information, and sound spirituality in concise, illustrative, readable, and eminently practical works on topics of current concern. Learning from stress; interior peace; personal prayer; biblical awareness; walking with others in darkness; appreciating the love already in our lives; spiritual discernment; uncovering helpful psychological antidotes for our tendency to worry too much at times; and important guides to improving interpersonal relations are only several of the areas which will be covered in this series.

The goal of each IlluminationBook, then, is to provide great ideas, helpful steps, and needed inspiration in small volumes. Each book offers a new beginning for the reader to explore possibilities and embrace practicalities which can be employed in everyday life.

In today's busy and anxious world, IlluminationBooks are meant to provide a source of support—without requiring an inordinate amount of time or prior preparation. Each small work stands on its own. Hopefully, the information provided not only will be nourishing in itself but also will encourage further exploration in the area.

One is obviously never done learning. With every morsel of wisdom each of these books provides, the goal is to keep the process of seeking knowledge ongoing even during busy times, when sitting down with a larger work is impossible or undesirable.

However, more than information (as valuable as it is), at the base of each work in the series is a deep sense of *hope* that is based on a belief in the beautiful statement made by Jesus to his disciples and in turn to us: "You are my friends" (Jn 15:15).

As "friends of God" we must seek the presence of the Lord in ourselves, in others, in silence and solitude, in nature, and in daily situations. IlluminationBooks are designed to provide implicit and explicit opportunities to appreciate this reality in new ways. So, it is in this spirit that this book and the other ones in the series are offered to you.                                        *—Robert J. Wicks*

*General Editor, IlluminationBooks*

The word *desert*—for the person who lets him or herself be taken up by the Spirit—expresses the search for God in silence. It is a "suspension bridge" thrown by the soul in love with God over the dark abyss of its own spirit, over the strange deep crevasses of temptation, over the unfathomable precipices of its own fears which form an obstacle to progress toward God.

—Carlo Carretto

# Introduction

*This is a book about living through our desert experiences. Each of us, at various times in our lives, have experiences of the desert. When I think of my own desert experiences, I think of the grief I felt after the death of my father, the difficulty I experienced while going through a major vocational change in my life, or the loneliness that I have sometimes felt when friends are far away. These have been times of dryness, times of aloneness. Like all desert experiences, they expressed the root meaning of the Latin word* desertus—*empty,* absent of living things. Perhaps our English word *deserted* captures this original meaning best.

When we experience the desert we feel alone, perhaps even abandoned or betrayed. These desert experiences are characterized by loss. It can be the loss of others brought on by death, alienation, relocation, or maybe for reasons that we cannot understand. The loss can also be a loss of our sense of ourselves. The familiar world that has made up our lives breaks down, and things don't make sense anymore. Often the loss of someone or something that has given meaning to our lives provokes such a crisis of identity for us. Or the loss can be the loss of God. The feelings of consolation we experienced at prayer may have evaporated. The God who was supposed to protect us from danger suddenly has failed us. Perhaps God just doesn't make sense anymore. All of these losses, whether of God, self, or others, drive us out of the familiar world into the desert.

There is a long tradition in Christian spirituality of associating difficult experiences with the desert. In the scriptures, the desert is a place of trial and testing. As Boniface Ramsey says:

> It is an environment in which most human beings find themselves either with reluctance and fear or with some strong and set purpose. In Christian terms, the desert stands for the arena in which one, while submitting to the test, meets one's spiritual salvation or spiritual doom. It is life itself in its starkest form. (Ramsey, p. 260)

Following in the footsteps of Jesus, Christians began to go out to the desert to begin a monastic life around the beginning of the fourth century. This movement led to the establishment of monasteries throughout the deserts of Palestine and Egypt. After the end of the Roman persecutions, Christians sought the glory of a new form of martyrdom—white martyrdom—of the desert, where they would confront the same ultimate trials of faith as their predecessors did.

Both the biblical and early monastic visions of the desert characterize it as a harsh and inhospitable place. The starkness of the desert is a place to meet temptation head on, where evil has no disguise to hide behind. In a similar way, our desert experiences challenge us to take stock of our lives, to look into the emptiness of our deserted hearts.

Unlike the early Christians, we do not go out to the desert to escape ordinary life, to live apart from an evil world. Cast into the desert by life's unexpected turns, our aim is simply to get out of the desert. For us, the desert is a place of transition, a place we seek to traverse and survive.

In this book I hope to share with you some of what I have learned from my own desert journeys and from those of others who have shared their experience with me. I have found that my own experience of the desert unfolds in four movements, which I reflect on in the four chapters of this book. The initial experience is one of being lost in a vast and hostile wilderness. But slowly, and often with great difficulty, we begin to find the strength to set out on a desert journey. As we cross the desert, we encounter various obstacles and setbacks,

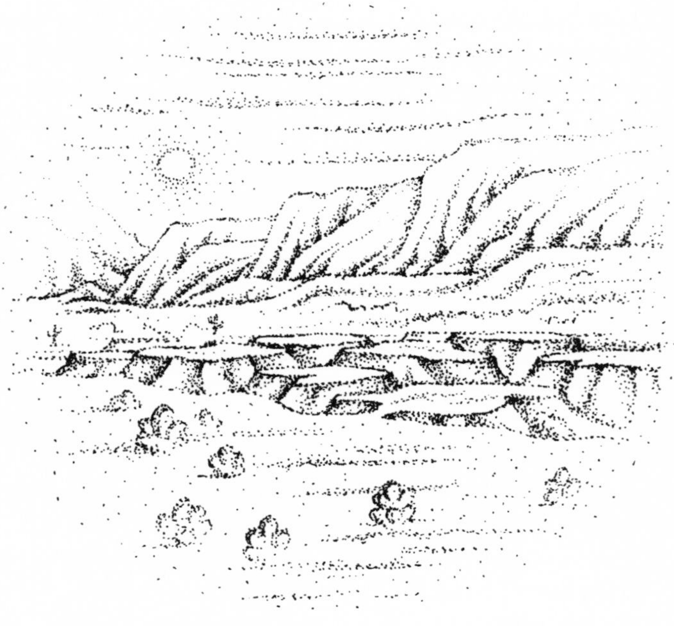

succumbing at times to the temptations we meet. Eventually, there is an end to our desert journey, but it is not usually the end that we had looked for. As we complete our desert journey, we find that we can't leave the desert entirely; it has become a part of us.

My journeys have taught me that while the interior desert can be a harsh place, it is not as deserted and hostile as it first appeared. Just as the earth's deserts reveal a subtle beauty to those with patience to watch and wait, so too do the deserts of our hearts. I hope the brief reflections and prayer suggestions offered in this book will not only help you find your bearings for your desert journey but also will open your eyes to the hidden presence of God.

**Chapter One**

# Lost in the Desert

**W**hat is it like to be lost in the desert?

I recall a story a priest told in a homily about his experience of being lost in the Arizona desert. Stationed in a city parish, he decided to see what it would be like to get out in the desert far from any traces of civilization. He set off in a Volkswagen microbus on a road he had heard would lead him into the middle of the desert. When the paved road ended, he continued on the dirt road. And when the dirt road ended, he decided to go a bit further, despite the fact that his old van was ill equipped for the journey.

It was hard to follow a straight course; he had to wend his way around rocks and rough terrain. But the desert was beautiful, with its tall saguaro cactus and its unusual rock formations. He turned off the engine and soaked up the peaceful silence while he ate a late lunch. There was no one around, just him, the rough desert floor below and the wide blue sky above.

Checking his watch and his fuel gauge, he decided that his curiosity was satisfied and that it was now time to turn around. But the journey back seemed longer than the journey out. As the sun settled toward the horizon, he noticed that his fuel gauge was now down to a quarter of a tank. He had already eaten what little food he had brought, and he had just a few ounces of water left. Concern began to grow into something he didn't yet want to name as fear.

That's when he discovered that the land up ahead dropped off into a deep canyon. There was no way around it. With real fear now, he knew he was lost. He had not passed any such canyon on the way out, and he had no idea where he was. In desperation, he decided to follow the rim of the canyon. There was no reason to believe that it would lead him out, but there was little else he could think of to do. He resisted the urge to drive more quickly, knowing he would only burn more fuel and perhaps end up breaking an axle.

As the sun began to set, he was down to an eighth of a tank. The canyon had flattened out now, and there was no reason to keep going on in this direction, but it seemed as good as any. As the sky darkened, he began to see the faint glow of city lights on the horizon to his left. He adjusted his course and bounced along as the needle began to flirt with the big *E* on the fuel gauge. He recalled that he had not told anyone of his plans for the day. And probably nobody would notice that he was missing until the next morning.

Pushing down thoughts of what he would do when his gas ran out, he rattled on. Then, to his amazement and relief, he saw up ahead the surface of a two-lane road. He met it at a sharp angle and followed it to the left, with the faint glow of the city just off to the right now. The needle rested firmly on *E*, but he drove on hopefully. Within a few miles, the road curved around a rocky hill and he saw ahead the lights of a gas station. Far from home and wildly off course, he was nevertheless safe. When he finally made it home, it was well past midnight.

\* \* \*

To be lost in the desert is a dangerous, fearful experience. The sense of isolation, of being alone in hostile territory can be overwhelming. If your car breaks down on a busy highway, it is natural to be afraid. Dependency on strangers is unsettling, and the potential for a violent encounter with a passerby is very real. But imagine the fear of being lost and alone in the middle of nowhere, with little hope of encountering anyone, friendly or hostile, for days.

Alone in the desert, you realize how small you are in the face of this vast expanse. There is just you and the sun. It beats down mercilessly, and there is no shade to be found. It is silent. Objects in the distance appear reachable, yet one can walk for an hour and be no closer. Attainable goals seem few and far between. At night, the sense of isolation can be even greater as a million stars shine down with a cold clarity. The realization of your smallness is inescapable, and the nearest person seems no closer than the brightest star.

In his poem "Desert Places" Robert Frost once wrote:

> They cannot scare me with their empty spaces,
> Between stars—on stars where no human race is
> I have it in me so much nearer home
> To scare myself with my own desert places.

While most of us have never actually experienced being lost in the desert, we have all, at times, felt lost. We have experienced the loss of self that comes with a crisis of meaning, the grief of losing another when a relationship ends or death occurs, and the desolation that befalls us when we can no longer find God. And these inner desert places can be as frightening as any real desert.

We do not expect to be lost in the desert. Like the priest who ventured out in his old microbus, we think we can handle whatever will come our way. We want to believe that we can plan our life's journey so that we can avoid the deserts completely. If we must pass through the desert, we plan to do so safely and securely, like people traveling in air-conditioned cars on an interstate. We never expect the paved roads of our lives to turn into dirt roads, or those dirt roads to lead us to the edge of the precipice.

Almost one-third of the earth's land surface is desert. Deserts are a part of the earth's ecology, part of the

# DANGER
# OPPORTUNITY

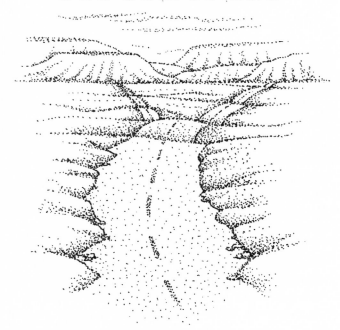

cycle of heating and cooling the atmosphere. Without deserts, there could be no lush rain forests, no verdant pastureland. So it is with the ecology of our lives. When our life's journey leads us into the desert, we are often unprepared—astonished and resentful that we should have to pass through this hostile territory, bewildered that we have lost our bearings. Yet without these deserts we cannot appreciate the green, fertile times in our lives.

To be lost in the desert is to confront a crisis. We often associate the notion of being in a crisis with a crossroads. When we come to a moment in our lives when we must choose between two options, we consider ourselves at a critical juncture. To borrow again from Robert Frost, we face "two roads...in a yellow wood."

As difficult as that sort of crisis can be, what we are confronting when we are "lost in the desert" is a different sort of crisis. There are not two roads before us; in fact there is no road at all. We feel disoriented, lost as to both where we are and how we came to be at this point. The Chinese word for *crisis* consists of two characters joined together. Individually the characters mean "danger" and "opportunity." This sense of the word *crisis* better reflects the situation we find ourselves in during these moments of being lost. We face a dangerous opportunity.

We are surrounded by danger. We question whether we will survive, whether we have the physical, emotional, and spiritual resources to withstand the onslaught before us. The dangers are clear, the opportunities are not. The only opportunity we can imagine is that perhaps, somehow, we will prevail. If we survive, we will be stronger for it. But as we stand alone in the midst of a wasteland, we're not thinking of it as a growth opportunity.

This type of crisis can have various forms. It can relate to the loss of another, or to the loss of God. But it also has a very personal dimension, and this may be what we feel most keenly. It is an experience of loss of self, and it occurs when the pattern, the order, the form that has given shape to our lives crumbles. Those things that have helped us make sense out of our lives are either out of reach, or if they are at hand, they just don't work any more.

Viktor Frankl, the German psychologist who survived Auschwitz, described this loss of meaning as a "vacuum." There is no air in a vacuum, and if the pressure on the outside is strong enough, it can crush the surrounding walls. In a vacuum of meaninglessness we feel as if the structure of our lives is as weak as an empty aluminum soda can. We find ourselves breathless, with the world around us closing in.

This experience of emptiness has nothing to do with our wants being satisfied. The very things that our culture puts so much emphasis on, like a comfortable home or a nice car, are not the things that give meaning to our lives. A sense of purpose, a desire to live a creative and caring life, someone to love and care for—these are the things that make our lives worthwhile. Indeed, all those immediate goals that once seemed so important seem quite empty when these larger purposes have been lost. Without an ultimate horizon in our lives, the objects in the foreground have little or no significance at all.

This crisis of meaning can have many causes. One of the most familiar is known as mid-life crisis. It is characterized by the recognition that our physical abilities are past their peak and by a confrontation with our mortality. At mid-life we tend to look back on what we have accomplished so far and recognize that all of our goals have not been met. We begin to accept that the time left to attain them is not unlimited and that some are no longer attainable. Perhaps we have not risen as high or as fast in our work as we had hoped, or if we have, our professional success has not brought the personal fulfillment that we expected. Peers, possibly even people younger than we, occasionally die. This recognition of limits leads us to reassess our goals, identity, and commitment.

While most people make some adjustments in their priorities, some find that what once gave meaning to their lives no longer does. Commitments crumble, careers change, friendships and family relationships are strained to the breaking point. It is not only the person in crisis who is affected, but also spouses, friends, and family.

While it often occurs during middle age, this type of crisis can happen at other times as well. Losing a job, being involved in a serious accident, undergoing a divorce, being a victim of a crime, suffering a serious illness, or the death of a parent or a friend—these are only some examples of the kinds of experiences that can be major sources of stress. At times the aftershocks can be strong enough to cause the foundations of our lives to shake and crumble. A crisis of meaning can occur at any age, at any time. Life keeps happening and things often fall apart.

Viktor Frankl offers this helpful description of what the experience is like: "Face to face with life's transitoriness we may say that the future does not yet exist; the past does not exist any more; and the only thing that really exists is the present" (Frankl, p. 102).

Such a crisis of meaning is well illustrated by the situation that the people of Israel faced during the flight from Egypt. They found themselves lost in the middle of the Sinai Desert without food, water, or any sense of where they were going. The Book of Exodus recounts two incidents where the people cried out in complaint against God.

The first was on the fifteenth day of the second month after their escape from Egypt. The whole people rose up in protest against Moses and Aaron saying, "If only we had died by the hand of the LORD in the land of Egypt, when we sat by our fleshpots and ate our fill of bread. For you have brought us out into the wilderness to kill this whole assembly with hunger" (Ex 16:2–3). The account of the second incident follows closely after this in Exodus 17. Here the people were in need of water, and once again they quarreled with Moses. "Why did you bring us out of Egypt, to kill us and our children and our livestock with thirst?" (Ex 17:3).

Frankl's description of crisis is a fitting one here. The past no longer exists, except as a memory. Just a little more than six weeks after God had inflicted ten plagues upon the Egyptians, divided the Red Sea for them to pass through, and destroyed the pursuing forces of pharaoh, the people had lost confidence. They didn't remember this. What they remembered was that no matter how hard life was back in Egypt, at least they had something to eat and drink.

When we find ourselves lost in the desert, our memory often becomes similarly distorted. We easily forget how, with God's help, we have handled previous crises. The past is not an empowering memory, but a haunting rebuke. We cry out "Why me?" or "If only this hadn't happened!" We have no confidence in ourselves and little or no sense of trust in God. Like the Israelites, we sometimes express our anger and desperation not to God directly, but to God's surrogates, be they friends, family, or those who minister to us.

If the past does not exist, neither does the future. To the Israelites in the desert, God's promise to lead them to a land flowing with milk and honey seemed like nothing but an illusion. It's as if they were saying to themselves, "How could we have been so stupid as to believe a promise like that?" Or perhaps it would be truer to the text to put it this way: "How could we have allowed ourselves to be duped by God? This whole thing was just a cruel trick, a ploy to bring us out to the desert to kill us."

In the midst of a crisis of meaning, life can indeed seem like a cruel trick, and God becomes a manipulative trickster. And we can only look upon ourselves with self-pity and perhaps even derision. We see ourselves as the most foolhardy of people, naive dreamers.

We have neither the past nor the future, only the present. And it beats down on us like the midday desert sun—harsh, unrelenting, inescapable. And we ask, "Is life worth living or not?" This is the ultimate question of faith. And how we answer determines whether our spirit dies there on the desert floor or we rise up to begin the journey.

*Psalm-prayer*

My God, my God, why have you forsaken me?
Why are you so far from helping me,
from the words of my groaning?
O my God, I cry by day, but you do not answer,
and by night, but find no rest.

I am poured out like water,
and all my bones are out of joint;
my heart is like wax;
it is melted within my breast;
my mouth is dried up like a potsherd,
and my tongue sticks to my jaws;
you lay me in the dust of death.

But you, O LORD, do not be far away!
O my help, come quickly to my aid!
Deliver my soul from the sword,
my life from the power of the dog!
Save me from the mouth of the lion!
                    *—Psalms 22:1–2, 14–15, 19–21*

*For reflection*

   • When have you experienced the desert in your life?

   • What were your feelings?

   • How did you feel about yourself?

   • About others?

   • Did your feelings toward God resonate with those of the psalmist?

## Chapter Two

# The Journey Begins

*T*he difference between being lost in the desert and being on a desert journey begins with desire. When we are lost, we are overwhelmed by the experience. We feel powerless to change our situation, and we can't imagine how life could ever return to normal. The God we have known is not there, and we cannot find God in this new set of circumstances. Even our sense of self may be lost.

It is natural in such a crisis to simply want the whole thing to just go away. But that is wishing for the impossible. Although this is a normal and perhaps even necessary reaction, as long as we remain at that point we will be lost, wandering aimlessly. At this stage a person who is lost will say, "There is nothing I can do. How can I go on?"

We move from hopelessness toward hope when we can say, "I do not know how I will go on, but I want to." When that desire breaks through the rubble of our shattered hopes, a new stage begins. We are no longer lost in the desert. We have begun our desert journey.

Where does this desire come from? Where do we get the strength for our desert journey? To say that it comes from God does not mean that we have no part in it. But neither can we say that we have to do it all on our own. That would be impossible. The presumption that we can handle the desert on our own is a very dangerous one, as the following story of Patrick Hodge illustrates.

Hodge was a forty-one-year-old adventurer who set out to test the limits of human endurance. He was fascinated by the desert and had made many hikes into it. In July 1991 he set out from Badwater, California, on a twenty-mile hike across Death Valley. He carried just three quarts of water.

Badwater is nearly the lowest point in North America—279 feet below sea level. The lowest point—282 feet—is just four miles to the west on the route that Hodge took. The temperature in Death Valley during July approaches 125 degrees. Zero percent humidity and a constant breeze can heat the ground to almost two hundred degrees. This was the terrain that Hodge sought to cross, ten miles each way.

Hodge told a friend that he was going to carry

only three quarts of water because he had figured out that it was the exact amount that he needed. His theory was that people set out carrying too much water and failed because the weight slowed them down. What Hodge had not anticipated was that in the midst of the desert there were salt pans, pools of water that, because of the high density of salt and other minerals, evaporate very slowly. He had not expected that these salt pans would leave behind a muddy terrain that would make walking much more difficult.

Despite this difficulty, and with just the three quarts of water, he still was able to make 19.5 miles of his 20-mile journey. He collapsed just one-half mile from his pickup. He apparently sat down to rest with his truck in sight. Exhausted, he collapsed and died of hyperthermia.

While we may not identify much with Patrick Hodge's reckless approach to life, especially when we are in the midst of a crisis, his story offers us an important caution. For when we find ourselves lost in the desert, we too may be inclined to take on a similar rugged-individualist attitude. We may try to steel ourselves against all the forces that surround us and attempt to make it on our own.

Some signs of this attitude are an unwillingness to talk about the crisis we are facing, resistance toward showing our emotions, and refusal to turn to God for help. We decide we can do it ourselves. When these attitudes are already in place when the crisis hits, they take root all the more firmly.

Such a person has desire in the heart, but it is a desire rooted in oneself rather than another. It is possible to survive a crisis with this attitude—but it is not possible to grow through the experience. Physical survival may not be an issue, unless one has any number of stress-related conditions. Perhaps psychological survival is possible too, although it would be hard to imagine such a person with the openness and vulnerability necessary to sustain a relationship beyond the immediate critical period. But spiritual survival is not possible. When one will not turn to God, will not cry out, even in desperation, for help, the spirit dies. It lies shriveled on the desert sand.

The story of Elijah fleeing Queen Jezebel serves as a counterpoint to the story of Patrick Hodge. It begins in 1 Kings 18 with Elijah's confrontation with the prophets of Baal. In a contest in which both sides call upon their god to bring down fire upon the sacrifice of a bull, Elijah shows that Baal is powerless. Jezebel is outraged and swears to kill him. Elijah flees for his life into the desert.

He goes a day's journey and then lies down in despair and says, "It is enough now, O LORD, take away my life." But God sends an angel to Elijah who awakens him from sleep. He places a small cake and water before Elijah and says "Get up and eat." Elijah eats and drinks, but then lies down and sleeps again. Once more the angel awakens him saying, "Get up and eat, otherwise the journey will be too much for you." And so strengthened by that meal, Elijah travels for forty days and forty nights through the desert to the mountain of God, Horeb (1 Kgs 19:4–8). In Exodus this same mountain is called Sinai.

It is probably easier for us to identify with Elijah than with Patrick Hodge. Like Elijah, we often feel

overwhelmed by the crises that confront us. Like Elijah, we often try to run from the difficult situations that we face. And when we feel like we can't go on anymore, we want to lie down and die.

After a day's journey into the wilderness, Elijah had no desire to go on. Had not the angel come, he certainly would have died there. But he did not die. The angel gave him food, which strengthened him. Although he had no desire of his own, God placed the desire in his heart. We might say that it was Elijah's complaint that saved him. "Let me die," he said. Even words such as these can be a prayer because, as lost and dejected as Elijah was, he still cried out to God. And God heard him.

God can do more with us when, from the midst of our helplessness, we cry out in despair than when we are determined to make it on our own. Lost in the desert, we cannot find God; God must find us. We have no desire of our own; God must place it within us. All we can do is cry out to God; our disconsolate, anguished cry is our only prayer.

The writer Jane Redmont relates how she cried out to God in just this way during a battle with severe depression and anxiety. In the midst of a panic attack, trembling with fear, she opened her Bible to the Psalms and began reading them aloud.

> I read aloud to steady myself, to keep the demons at bay, to make the words more real and hold them in my mouth. At last I was able to cry. The psalms gave words to my heart and even to my

body. "O LORD, heal me," says Psalm 6, "for my bones are shaking with terror, while you, O LORD—how long?" (Redmont, p. 15)

Our journey through the wilderness likewise begins when we cry out for help. The psalms can indeed give voice to our lament. Like the psalmist we can cry out:

How long, O LORD? Will you forget me forever?
How long will You hide your face from me?
(Ps 13:1)

When we are lost in the desert, we often find that what used to work for us in prayer no longer does. Our ability to concentrate is often the first thing to go. And with it goes meditation and contemplation. We may find ourselves reverting to the simplest prayers we know, the prayers of our childhood. Or perhaps we may just repeat a word or a phrase over and over, feeling like nothing is happening and God is far away.

While it is always important to refrain from judging our prayer by the quality of our ability to stay focused or by the feelings of enlightenment and consolation it brings us, this is particularly crucial during these desert periods. Once we engage in this type of evaluation of the quality of our prayer, we will undoubtedly come to the conclusion that it is not as good as it once was or should be. There will be little sense of God, and so it is dangerously easy to conclude that God is not there.

But all the while we are seeking God, God is seeking us. Jane Redmont, in her article, "Praying in Times of

Depression," says that although she could not meditate any more, "Still God was present, and I knew it. I did not face the fear alone. Yet the way I prayed underwent a profound change" (p. 15). Instead of relying on her own ability to pray, she began to turn to friends in a new way. She speaks of calling friends in the midst of a desperate moment and asking them to pray for her; she discovers that while she cannot meditate alone, she can pray when she allows another to guide her in meditation.

We too may find ourselves foraging for new ways to pray in the midst of the desert. Like the many creatures who live there, we find ourselves pressed to adapt, to learn how to live with less, to move about in the cool of the night out of the menacing sun. Perhaps we will find new ways to meet God. It may be music, the rosary, or the Jesus prayer, or maybe just a quiet walk.

One of the clearest signs of God's presence in crisis is the care and concern of friends. Friends usually want to help us, and some friends know well how to do that even without our asking. With these friends, all we have to do is allow them to help. It's simply a matter of accepting their love without resistance and appreciating what they do for us. Other friends may want to help, but they're too hesitant to offer. Or perhaps they are going about it in the wrong way, doing things that make us uncomfortable or irritate us. We simply need to let them know. We may want to tell them what to avoid doing and ask them to do what we think would really help us. They will probably be more than happy to oblige.

Lost in the desert, friends can be to us what the

angel was to Elijah. They revive us and nourish us, reminding us that we do not make the journey alone. They are God's way of putting the desire back in our heart. They can't take us out of the desert, but they can get us to stand up and walk. And they can accompany us on the journey.

Barry Lopez is a nature writer who seeks to allow his communion with the land to teach him. In a little book called *Desert Notes* he reflects on his experience in the desert and how it resists his attempts to understand it. "The land does not give easily. The desert is like a boulder; you expect to wait" (Lopez, p. 7).

So it is with our desert journeys. We want our personal deserts to yield to our attempts to turn them into gardens. But they do not change. They are as hard as boulders. We must wait. "You can't get at it this way," Lopez says. "You must come with no intentions of discovery....You have to proceed almost by accident."

What is it like for us to be on a desert journey "with no intentions of discovery"? What is it like "to proceed almost by accident"? It means that, like Elijah, we simply get up and start walking. Elijah's journey of "forty days and forty nights" is symbolic of the long way he had to go, both externally and interiorly. The text calls our attention to the length of time of the journey and thus alerts us to the fact that there is more going on here than just covering a certain amount of ground. That it took so long meant that Elijah did not go by the most direct route. If he had walked in a straight line, he would have gotten there much sooner. But as he began to walk through the Sinai wilderness, he did not know where he was going, and so he did not know the way. Nor could he have known how long the journey would take. He proceeded "with no intentions of discovery...almost by accident."

Almost, but not entirely. He carried within him the memory of the angel who had nurtured him. He carried the desire God had planted in his heart. And so, while he wandered, he discovered only at the end that his wandering was not in vain. The memory sustained him. Whereas the people of Israel were lost in the desert because of their forgetfulness, Elijah was guided because of his memory. When we are wandering in the desert, we too are guided by the memory that God has helped us in the past.

This awareness can help us in our prayer. Jane Redmont tells how the memory of Jesus' love for others sustained her in prayer:

> I said with all my strength, "Jesus, I don't usually ask you for much, but I'm asking you now, in the name of all those people you healed, in the name of the man born blind and the bent-over woman and the woman who bled for years, in the name of the man with demons and the little girl you raised up, HELP ME." (Redmont, p. 16)

Even when we cannot remember God's love, we can pray in the name of others we know who believe, be they family, friends, or the saints.

Although Elijah finds no answers on the way, he

discovers them at the end, when he reaches the holy mountain. Upon the mountain God is revealed to him, but not in the manner he expects. First he experiences a powerful wind, then an earthquake, and then a fire. But God is not to be found in any of these. It is only in the silence of a gentle breeze that he meets God.

On our desert journeys we too must proceed without looking for answers. There is no promise of answers at the end. Nor is there any timeline. We can't make one for ourselves, and we should resist if others try to put us on one. All we can know is that it takes time. We can do this only if we remember what we have lost and what we are looking for. An answer will not bring back what has been lost. And only God can satisfy our heart's longing.

So what should we do? Counselors often advise people suffering from depression that the best thing to do is to be active, to get involved in something. This takes their minds off themselves and gets them focused outwardly again.

The same is true of us on our desert journeys. The desert journey is a Christian journey, and the point of Christianity is not to dwell on oneself, but to love and serve others. When we find ourselves in the desert, we might divert our attention from our own experience by doing something for others. Perhaps we don't have the energy to do very much. Then do just one little thing for somebody else. It's not a question of joining a committee or of dedicating large blocks of time. Just take it one step at a time. Listen to the direction that your heart draws you in and go that way.

These actions are not only expressions of Christian love, they are also expressions of faith and hope. Faith is not just believing, but putting one's beliefs into practice. So too, hope is not just being optimistic, but acting in a way that reflects one's trust in the future. By acting in a faithful and hopeful way, we begin to create meaning where none has existed.

The psychologist Sharon Parks has written about this connection between faith and meaning. She points out that by engaging in creating meaning in the midst of meaningless situations, we are actually acting in faith. To have faith is to act faithfully, to do as God would do, even if God seems far from us.

> It is in the activity of finding and being found by meaning that we as modern persons come closest to recognizing our participation in the life of faith. It is in the activity of composing and being composed by meaning, then, that I invite the reader to associate with the word faith. (Parks, pp. 13–14)

As we compose the meaning of our desert journey, we are in turn composed by it.

"All the way to God is God," St. Catherine of Siena once wrote. I think that what she meant was that while we are looking for God but not finding God, God is already there in our searching. The very act of looking, the weak and imperfect prayer that we make, even the lament we cry is the work of the Spirit within us. The French writer Blaise Pascal put it this way: "You would not be searching for me unless you had already found me."

*Psalm-prayer*

O God, you are my God, I seek you,
my soul thirsts for you;
my flesh faints for you,
as in a dry and weary land
where there is no water.

As a deer longs for flowing streams,
so my soul longs for you, O God.
My soul thirsts for God, for the living God.
When shall I come and behold the face of God?
My tears have been my food day and night,
while people say to me continually, "Where is
your God?"

These things I remember, as I pour out my soul:
how I went with the throng,
and led them in procession to the house of God,
with glad shouts and songs of thanksgiving,
a multitude keeping festival.
Why are you cast down, O my soul,
and why are you disquieted within me?
Hope in God; for I shall again praise him,
my help and my God.

*–Psalms 63:1; 42:1–6*

*For reflection*

    • Where have you found the desire to begin your desert journey?

    • How has your prayer changed as you pass through the desert? What kind of prayer is best for you?

    • Who have you turned to for help? What kinds of things that others have done have been most helpful to you?

    • What memories of God's presence sustain you in the desert? What does faith mean to you as you make your desert journey?

**Chapter Three**

# Crossing the Desert

*T*he desert is a place we pass through on the way to somewhere else. Few of us imagine ourselves living in the desert, and those of us who do have pretty much tamed it. Nevertheless, we recognize the limits of our ability to control nature and remain wary of desert crossings.

The Old and New Testaments are rooted in a desert environment. Both the writers and hearers of the ancient biblical stories knew the desert well. Even city-dwellers in Jerusalem or Jericho were within a short distance of the desert. They needed no cautions about the dangers of desert travel and understood well both the natural and human dangers that a crossing presented.

So it is not surprising that the symbol of the desert loomed large in their religious imaginations. It was, first and foremost, the place of Israel's deliverance. God led the chosen people out of slavery through the desert into the freedom of the promised land. God led Israel through the desert, guiding them with a cloud by day and a pillar of fire by night. There God provided manna to eat and made water flow from the rock to quench their thirst.

But the desert was also the place where Israel's hardness of heart was manifested. It was, as we saw earlier, at Massah and Meribah that Israel tested God, complaining bitterly and crying out in anger. This intransigence was memorialized in Psalm 95 as a caution to succeeding generations:

> Oh that today you would listen to his voice!
> Do not harden your hearts, as at Meribah,
> as on the day at Massah in the wilderness.
> (Ps 95:7–8)

The desert was a place of transition for Israel, both politically and spiritually. In the desert they were forged into a nation, liberated by God from the slavery of Egypt and guided into the promised land. These powerful images of slavery and freedom functioned not only on a political level but on the spiritual level as well. It was in the forty years of wandering that God softened their hearts and taught them to listen. It was a spiritual transition from hardness of heart to receptivity and obedience of heart.

Jesus would have known all this very well. It would have been somewhere in his mind when, after his baptism, "the Spirit immediately drove him out into the wilderness" (Mk 1:12). As he went into the desert, he may have carried with him the awareness that this was to be a time of transition. Something was being left behind and something new lay ahead. The Spirit had come upon him, and his private life in Nazareth was now behind him. What was ahead may not have been at all clear. But Jesus went out into the desert to prepare his heart to listen to the voice of the God he would call Abba—dear father or daddy. He went out to become receptive to the leading of the Spirit who guided him.

As we proceed beyond the beginnings of our desert journey, we become aware that we are making a crossing. Something has been left behind—perhaps a loved one who is no longer with us, perhaps a group of friends whose support is no longer available, perhaps a way of life that accompanied a particular vocation or job. As we move away from the separation, we carry that pain of parting in our hearts. We bring the memory of what once was with us. But we are also aware of a certain finality.

We can't go back there again. We're on our way to somewhere else. We may not be moving physically at all, but we are on a journey whose destination is not clear. We go forward hesitantly, haltingly feeling our way.

People begin to call us by new names. We go from married to divorced, from professional to unemployed, from wife to widow, from well to sick. But the new name is not part of who we are. It's more like a pointer to where we are going, much like the "promised land" was merely a name that the Israelites used for some unknown country that lay ahead. Our new name often fits uncomfortably. It provides little help in getting us to where we are going.

We are in a liminal land. We're not sure who we are, and it doesn't even matter that much. We're more interested in surviving. We know that we can't quit the journey. There's nowhere to stop in the desert. We may encounter an occasional oasis, but after a brief drink, the pools of water evaporate before our eyes, as if they were an optical illusion.

Thomas Merton once described the desert fathers and mothers of early Christianity as having made "a clean break with the conventional, accepted social context in order to swim for [their lives] into an apparently irrational void." In the midst of the desert, we have become like these ancient ascetics. They fled from civilization on a deliberately spiritual quest. We have probably not embraced our desert experience freely, as they did, nor did we intend to enter into a spiritual quest. But willing or not, we find ourselves in the midst of the desert, struggling for our very lives.

We don't know who we will become, but we are learning how to work on the project. The French writer Léon Bloy said, "Suffering enters into the human heart and creates a space where nothing was before." As we proceed on our desert journey, we discover that we are indeed moving into an empty space in our hearts and begin to fill it in. If we take a look at Jesus' desert sojourn, his crossing from the old to the new, perhaps it can enlighten our own. What temptations did he face? What survival skills did he need? What can this teach us?

Jesus' three temptations in his desert are well known: to turn stones into bread, to throw himself down from the pinnacle of the temple to be rescued by angels, and to worship Satan in exchange for all the kingdoms of the world. They were not just temptations for those forty desert days but a foreshadowing of what lay ahead in his ministry. So too, our trials during our desert crossings indicate the tests we will see again later.

The first temptation is really the most straightforward and obvious. "He fasted forty days and forty nights, and afterward he was famished," Matthew tells us. The Tempter says, "If you are the Son of God, command these stones to become loaves of bread" (Mt 4:2–3). This is a temptation to ease the pain of hunger. Jesus went out to the desert to fast and is tested to break the fast. Fasting is not just a means of self-denial, but of sharpening one's senses to hear, to see, to feel God. To break the fast would be to defeat the very reason Jesus went into the desert. He might just as well leave the desert as stay there and not fast.

Turn the stones into bread. Make the hunger go away. Dissolve the suffering of the desert. This is the first temptation we face on our desert crossing too. "The desert is like a boulder," Barry Lopez says. "You expect sometime it will loosen into pieces to be examined. When it doesn't, you weary." We don't have the power to change the desert boulder into bread. We can either stay and wait or we can run.

We run from the desert when we eat the hollow bread of complacency and denial. We can indulge ourselves saying, "After all I've been through, I deserve it." Food, alcohol, sleeping pills, casual sex...there are many ways to bury the pain. These things will make us feel better, at least for a while. But they won't get us across the desert. They will eventually leave us depleted, lying flat on our faces in the relentless desert sun, perhaps too exhausted to get up. The real hunger doesn't go away. We have nowhere to hide from it, no shade to run to. Running quickly exhausts us. We can't hide in our own shadow.

This is not the way. We must stay and confront whatever it is that has driven us to the desert to begin with. The very thing we want to run from will eventually kill us if we do not face it. It's like the rattlesnake you come upon in the desert. If you run, it will spring at you. Lopez says, "What makes you want to leave now is what is trying to kill you....Have patience until the rattlesnake kills itself."

"One does not live by bread alone, but by every word that comes from the mouth of God" (Mt 4:4), Jesus replies to the Tempter. Only God can sustain us in our desert crossing. We have not the strength. With the psalmist we cry out:

> My soul languishes for your salvation;
> I hope in your word.
> Your word is a lamp to my feet
> and a light to my path. (Ps 119:81, 105)

The second temptation places Jesus at the height of the temple, with the Tempter challenging him to throw himself down. Jesus had quoted scripture after the first temptation, and so the Tempter now quotes it back to him:

> He will command his angels concerning you....
> On their hands they will bear you up,
> so that you will not dash your foot against a stone.
> (Ps 91:11–12)

This is a temptation to test God, as the Israelites had done in the desert. Like the previous temptation, it challenged Jesus to use power to obtain his ends. It was a temptation Jesus faced often in ministry, not only from his opponents, who demanded a sign to prove that he was the Messiah, but also from his disciples, who wanted him to bring about the reign of God with power and might and to place them in glory with him. But Jesus would not use power to bring about God's reign. His was the way of the powerless. His way led not to political or military victory, but to the cross.

As we make our desert crossing, we are not deluded into thinking that we have the power to make the pain go away. We have learned that we can no more heal ourselves than we can make a stone turn to bread. We cannot put a life back together that has been irreparably shattered. Since we are keenly aware of our powerlessness, our temptation differs from that of Jesus. We don't have any power to work with, so we are inclined to maximize whatever little bit of leverage we think we have with God. We try to make a deal, to strike a bargain with God.

> "God, if you do this, then I'll...."
> "If you heal me, I'll go to Mass every day."
> "If you change Joe, I'll go back to him."
> "If you get me that job, I'll give ten percent of my salary to the poor."

God doesn't seem to respond well to such offers. Such deals place God in the position of being a power broker, and God doesn't seem to like that. These paltry offers on our part are, in a sense, an accusation against God. They're like saying, "God, you're the one who put me in this mess, now what's it gonna take for you to get me out of it?"

The false assumption we make is that God did this to us. God sent the disease; God took someone away; God caused the accident; etc. "Well," you may argue, "if God didn't do it then why did it happen?" We'll probably never get an adequate answer to this question. While we may go on asking it, simply because we have to, we should also look within ourselves and ask, "Why is it that I need this answer so desperately? Why am I still clinging to what I need to let go of? Why do I want to blame God?"

The Tempter tried to trick Jesus into believing in a God who would provide a quick fix, an easy out. We confront that same temptation. For us, it's not a matter of throwing ourselves down from the heights to be caught by an angel, but of holding an ultimatum up to God. "Fix it," we say, "and then I'll believe."

Jesus responds, "Do not put the Lord your God to the test" (Mt 4:7). God does not offer quick fixes. God does not provide detailed explanations. God does not respond to ultimatums.

Who is this God? The Tempter's third test offers Jesus a God who is easy to believe in: "Again the devil took him to a very high mountain and showed him all the kingdoms of the world and their splendor; and he said to him, 'All these I will give you if you fall down and worship me'" (Mt 4:8-9). On one level, this seems like a ridiculous temptation. Jesus recognizes the devil for who he is. Why would he worship him?

But on a more subtle level we can look at this as a temptation to fashion a God of our own making, a God who fits with our limited understanding. This is what the Israelites did when they fashioned a golden calf and worshiped it on their desert crossing. The Tempter offers Jesus power, adulation, earthly kingdoms. This is what Jesus' disciples often wanted him to do. Their arguments over who would sit at his right hand in glory reveal just such an expectation. It's also what Pilate and Herod presumed Jesus was after. But as Jesus said to Pilate, "My kingdom is not from this world" (Jn 18:36).

The heart of this issue is not *where* the kingdom is, but *what kind* of kingdom it is and *how* it comes. Jesus' passion and death reveal a kingdom that does not come by power, but by powerlessness; not by conquest, but by the cross. "Away with you, Satan....Get behind me Satan," Jesus responds.

On our desert crossings we face the same temptation when we want to fashion a God who is like us. Theologian Catherine Mowry LaCugna puts it this way: "If we think that by our own efforts or our own ideas we have found GOD, we may have 'found' just a product of our own imaginations, or needs, or wishful thinking." She quotes Ruth Burrows, a Carmelite sister, who says:

> We want our own version of [God], one we can, so to speak, carry around in our pockets rather as some superstitious people carry around a charm. We can hold endless, loving conversations with this one, feel we have an intimate understanding with him, we can tell him our troubles, ask for his approbation and admiration, consult him about all our affairs and decisions and get the answer we want, and this god of ours has almost nothing to do with the real God.

It's not always easy to tell the difference between a god of our own making and the true, living God. We may think of God as our protector, or cling to God as a source of surety. But tragedies and crises in our lives can challenge such convictions. In the face of this challenge we can simply deny our doubts and bolster our image of God with new arguments and explanations, or we can allow ourselves to be open to the unknown, to come to a new and unforeseen awareness of God. As LaCugna says, "God who dwells in light inaccessible exceeds every concept and image we have of God, else God would not be GOD" (Martin, p. 21).

As we make our desert crossing, we cannot find such a God. Rather, God finds us. The fact that we have embarked on this journey is an indication of already having been found. As we continue our search for the One who is always in search of us, there are certain desert skills that can be helpful.

Of the many survival skills necessary for our desert crossings, the ability to listen attentively and see clearly can be most important. Without such skills, we can easily fall victim to the many temptations we face.

When we first enter the desert, it seems as if there is little to see or hear. It appears to our untrained eyes as a silent, empty wasteland. And in comparison to our experience of contemporary life in cities and suburbs, it is indeed quiet and vacant. There are no people—the drone of automobiles, the constant sound of radios, the clatter of background noise are gone. Nor are there the more familiar soothing sounds we are accustomed to in our usual places of refuge, in parks or the quiet of our gardens. There are no birds singing, no leaves rustling, no crickets chirping.

The desert is quiet, but not completely silent. As we become accustomed to its rhythms, we begin to perceive its more subtle sounds. We begin to discover the many life-forms that the desert does sustain and to hear the faint noises they make. At night, many more come out for us to hear, though they usually are too elusive for us to see. What we hear most readily and most often is the sound of the wind, persistently and eternally carving the contours of this quiet, sparse land.

While at first glance there is apparently little to see in the desert, after a while we begin to notice things. What initially seemed like a barren uniformity gradually comes into focus. We discover a rich variety of plant life–piñon pines, sagebrush, cactus, various succulents. We may not know their names, but we begin to distinguish among them. And the land begins to reveal a complexity of shapes and forms. What at first just seemed rough now displays a rich diversity of texture and color. And we begin to examine not only the objects in our view but the clarity of the air, the sharpness of our vision, the bright visibility of the desert light.

The desert teaches us to listen and to see. The early Christian desert dwellers knew this well. They went not only to escape the cities but to allow the desert to refine their ability to pay attention to God. Wendy Wright says of them:

> Only in the stillness of a single, focused attention, they felt, could they sift through the myriad, conflicting voices that crowd the human heart....We, too, have an urgent need to ferret out the small, still whisper of divine prompting that so easily gets submerged in the rowdy chorus of voices that clamor for our attention each day. To listen deeply, to listen with a tender, yielding heart; to listen adventurously enough to be utterly surprised by what we hear—this we all need to be able to do. (Wright, p. 7)

This is especially so as we make our desert crossings. Just as the desert refines our perceptive abilities, our inner desert experience calls on us to develop the survival skill that the Christian tradition terms discernment. Discernment is the ability to sort through the many interior and exterior voices to discover which ones will lead us in the life-giving direction of God's loving will.

The ancient desert mothers and fathers often referred to these "voices" as "spirits." We are less likely to attribute our inner urgings to the work of warring spirits, schooled as we are in the language of psychology and values. Nevertheless, like them we must grapple with the conflicting demands and needs we face, especially as we negotiate our way through a painful transition in our lives. And unlike them, we must strive to do this while we live lives that can be unbearably complicated by the daily demands of work, family, and friendship. We who are "in the world" need to find our own desert refuge where we can discover the constant presence of the Spirit, that Wind of God who is persistently and eternally shaping the contours of our lives.

The process of discernment requires faith. Robert Wicks puts it this way:

> Discernment is a spiritual movement in which we try to decide who God is "calling" us to be and what we are asked to do in specific instances, now and in the future. Without grace, without God, there is (by definition) no process of discernment. (Wicks, p. 11)

One of the hard-won realizations of coming this far on our desert journey is the belief that we are not alone, that God is with us. Just as we found the strength in God to pick ourselves up off the desert floor and begin our journey, we also find the ability to listen and watch with faith for the signs of God's guiding Spirit in our lives.

The Letter to the Hebrews speaks of the faith of our ancestors, who had the courage to move forward trusting that God would lead them. One such ancestor was Moses, who led the Israelites on their desert crossing. The author of Hebrews writes about Moses, "By faith he left Egypt, unafraid of the king's anger; for he persevered as though he saw him who is invisible" (Heb 11:27). This is exactly the kind of faith that a desert crossing teaches us. We learn to see, to judge, to act according to the definition of faith that Hebrews provides: "the assurance of things hoped for, the conviction of things not seen" (Heb 11:1).

For us to "walk by faith" is to move forward with sometimes hesitant steps but with the confidence that the God who already has found us is a God of life. God has not brought us out to the desert to let us die there. God does will life for us. But only through a process of discernment can we identify those inner desires and longings that do lead to the peace and joy of God's reign.

Discernment requires an interior freedom. It is a process in which we simultaneously seek to own our innermost desires and yet not to cling to them. It requires an openness on our part that makes us very vulnerable. James

Fenhagen points out that sometimes what is most difficult to let go of is not our heart's longing, but our cherished hurts:

> The process of transformation is not without pain. In becoming open to all that is new, there is the pain of letting go of all that is old. Sometimes the things that hurt the most are the hardest to discard. The promise, however, is that in the struggle—the ongoing, ever changing struggle for growth—God is always present. (Quoted in Wicks, p. 12)

As we struggle with the process of discernment, we begin to see that we must relinquish many of the illusions and delusions that we carry about God and about ourselves. The desert is infamous for mirages. On our desert crossings we are frequently challenged by the many mirages that appear. We want to run toward them, but they are illusory. The god of the escape from pain, the god of the quick fix, the god just like me—these are mirages, phantoms that will vanish even as we grasp at them. We must likewise allow delusions about ourselves to melt away. We are neither self-reliant trailblazers nor helpless victims.

We need to go to our desert refuge, where we can discover who we are. There, as we sit patiently in the loving gaze of God, we can begin to discover our uniqueness. There the unfocused anonymity of our wounded self gradually comes into the clarity of God light. What at first seemed barren and useless reveals a rare complexity that, had it not been for this desert light, might have remained undiscovered.

*Psalm-prayer*

In you, O LORD, I seek refuge;
do not let me ever be put to shame;
in your righteousness deliver me.
Incline your ear to me; rescue me speedily.
Be a rock of refuge for me,
a strong fortress to save me.

You are indeed my rock and my fortress;
for your name's sake lead me and guide me,
take me out of the net that is hidden for me,
for you are my refuge.
Into your hand I commit my spirit;
you have redeemed me, O LORD, faithful God.

You hate those who pay regard to worthless idols,
but I trust in the LORD.
I will exult and rejoice in your steadfast love!

*—Psalms 31:1–7*

*For reflection*

&bull; As you make your desert journey, what have you left behind? What is the new name that you are called by? How do you feel about this?

&bull; What kind of space has suffering created in your heart? With what do you want to fill this space?

• What aspect of your desert journey makes you want to abandon it? Where are you tempted to go?

• What bargains do you try to strike with God as you make your desert crossing? What ultimatums do you offer God?

• What is the difference between the "god" you want to fashion and the real God?

## Chapter Four

# At Home in the Desert

*I*s there an end to our desert journey? How will we know it is over?

Before we attempt to offer some answers to these questions, we should recognize the significance of even asking them. We should remember where we have come from.

There was a time when we were lost in the desert, but we are no longer. We have found the courage to begin our journey, and despite many wrong turns on the way, we have made progress. We no longer say, "Why should I try to stand up and walk?" or even "How can I go on?" We have learned how to travel in the desert. We have come to recognize its signposts, and we walk on. It is not a question of survival, but of how long we will go on like this.

Is there an end to our desert journey? In one sense, there is. We gradually come out of the arid waste-land into a more fertile and friendly terrain. Our hearts mend, we find new purpose, we learn to love again. But in another sense, we never leave the desert behind, having adapted ourselves to a desert environment. We have grown familiar with its rhythms and cycles. We've come to respect the hardy creatures who live in its sparse environment. Like the cactus, we've learned to store water to last between the long rainfalls. We've learned to live with what the desert gives. It has become a permanent part of us.

We have seen the prophecy of Isaiah fulfilled in us: "In the wilderness, prepare the way of the LORD, make straight in the desert a highway for our God" (Is 40:3). Suffering has entered into our hearts and made a space for God there. The Lord has prepared a highway through the barren desert of our lives. The Lenten desert has become the Advent desert.

The Navajo people, like all Native Americans, place a high value on listening to the land. Harmony with their physical surroundings is an essential part of their religious belief. As a desert people, they have come to appreciate the subtle beauty of their homeland and have learned to live in a way that is sensitive to the grandeur of the desert and respectful of the fragile and diverse life-forms that exist there. The Navajo word for this experience of harmony is *hozro*. For them, living in harmony with their surroundings is not only a matter of survival, it is also a

recognition of the constant presence of the divine mystery in their lives.

Our desert journey has taught us to listen to the landscape of our hearts as well. Whatever the hurt, whatever the brokenness, whatever the loss, we have discovered that we cannot survive if we deny it or run from it. Just as the desert cannot be tamed, we cannot master our pain. We have begun to learn to live with it, to make it a companion of sorts. As we befriend our woundedness, we discover the presence of God there. We recognize it as a source of the divine mystery in our lives and bring ourselves into harmony, into *hozro*, with it.

When we have learned this harmony, the journey is over. We are no longer trying to get out of the desert, we are at home there. "I will set in the desert the cypress," Isaiah says, "so that all may consider and understand that the hand of the LORD has done this" (Is 41:19–20). We who once could only survive beside the running streams now flourish in arid lands. We become a sign of God's loving-kindness in the midst of the wilderness. The desert is no longer a place of desolation and abandonment, but of consolation and presence.

We see this same dynamic in the life of Jesus. The desert was first a place of trial and temptation for him. But having confronted the devil in the desert, he was free to return there and to make it a place of refuge. Time and again the gospels narrate how Jesus went out to the desert to pray when his disciples did not grasp his message or when the crowds pressed him for signs and wonders. They confronted him with the very same temptations he had faced earlier. Having faced those temptations in the desert, Jesus could return to the desert when they pressed him again. But on his return they were not so powerful. They were no longer strangers, but familiar companions. The place where he was tested severely became a refuge for him. The place where he confronted the evil one became a place to encounter the presence of Abba.

Jesus learned to be at home in the desert. He learned how to face his vulnerabilities and to live in peace with them. This is not to say that there was no struggle or anxiety. Certainly the scene in the garden of Gethsemane testifies to the struggle that Jesus faced. But in saying yes to God in the midst of his struggle, Jesus learned to allow the healing presence of the Spirit to console and strengthen him.

Just as the desert was a part of Jesus' life even until the end, so it is for us. The memory of the loss is always there, and it can reemerge in unexpected ways. Sometimes these memories will be a source of pain, but at other times they can be a source of courage. When we remember what the Lord has done for us, our scars are reminders of the dangerous yet wondrous desert crossing that we made. The suffering of the desert time becomes for us, as it was for Jesus and the Israelites before him, a reminder of God's presence.

Only when we have learned to survive the harshness of the desert can we come to appreciate its beauty. Carlo Carretto recognized this well. He left a successful career as an educator in post-war Italy to join a religious community. He became a member of the Little Brothers of Jesus, a community founded by Charles de Foucauld that stressed the hidden life of Jesus in Nazareth as a model for monastic living. Carretto went to live in a remote Arab village in the Sahara desert and sought to be a sign of Christ's presence there among its Muslim inhabitants.

This brief excerpt, one of his many reflections on his life in the desert, expresses the beauty of the desert and, in particular, the wonder of the night sky:

> How often, lying wrapped on a blanket in the sand, have I passed hour after hour gazing at a starry dome ceaselessly speaking to me, questioning me, helping me to find my bearings in the dark!
>
> Why do we live?
>
> Why do things come to be?
>
> Why do I plod along like a wandering shepherd?
>
> Why this vast silence?
>
> Why do the stars look down as though indifferent to our suffering?
>
> Withal, one thing is certain, this light, the sign of the truth we seek and the means by which we may catch a glimpse of it, has not got its roots on earth. Light comes from up there, it comes from something stretching above me, something transcending me, something preceding me.

Like Carretto, we have come to appreciate the ways that the desert ceaselessly speaks to us, constantly questions us, and gradually teaches us to find our way, even in the dark. We do not possess the answers, and we have learned not to look to God as some great answer in the sky. Rather, like the brilliant light of the desert stars, God stretches before us, bears us up, yet transcend us. God goes before us through the desert, offering not an answer, but an invitation, bidding us to come and follow.

*Psalm-prayer*

When the poor and needy seek water,
and there is none,
and their tongue is parched with thirst,
I the LORD will answer them,
I the God of Israel will not forsake them.

I will open rivers on the bare heights,
and fountains in the midst of the valleys;
I will make the wilderness a pool of water,
and the dry land springs of water.

I will put in the wilderness the cedar,
the acacia, the myrtle, and the olive;
I will set in the desert the cypress,
the plane and the pine together,

so that all may see and know,
and may consider and understand,
that the hand of the LORD has done this,
the Holy One of Israel has created it.
                              *–Isaiah 41:17–20*

*For reflection*

     • What kind of end to your desert journey do you hope for?

     • Is there a sense in which you have come to be at home in the desert?

     • What has the desert taught you? About yourself? About others? About God?

# References and Resources

Arritt, Susan. *The Living Earth Book of Deserts.* Pleasantville, N.Y.: Reader's Digest, 1993.

Benyo, Richard. "A Death in the Valley," *Los Angeles Magazine* 37, no. 8 (August 1992): pp. 52–58.

Carretto, Carlo. *Selected Writings,* ed. Robert Ellsberg. Maryknoll, N.Y.: Orbis Books, 1994.

Frankl, Viktor. *The Unheard Cry for Meaning.* New York: Simon and Schuster, Touchstone Books, 1978.

Lopez, Barry. *Desert Notes, River Notes.* New York: Avon Books, 1990.

Martin, James. "How Can I Find God?" *America* 173, no. 9 (September 30, 1995): pp. 12–21.

Parks, Sharon. *The Critical Years, The Young Adult Search for a Faith to Live By.* San Francisco: Harper and Row, 1986.

Ramsey, Boniface. "Desert," in *The New Dictionary of Catholic Spirituality*, ed. Michael Downey. Collegeville, Minn.: The Liturgical Press, 1993.

Redmont, Jane. "Praying in a Time of Depression," *America* 173, no. 5 (August 26, 1995): pp. 14–20.

Wicks, Robert. *Living Simply in An Anxious World*. Mahwah, N.J.: Paulist Press, 1988.

Wright, Wendy. "Desert Listening," *Weavings* 9, no. 3 (May–June, 1994): pp. 6–16.

**ILLUMINATIONBOOKS**

## Other Books in the Series